broken words/better days

Fyrn Vosshall

BookLeaf Publishing

India | USA | UK

Presentation by *BookLeaf Publishing*

Web: www.bookleafpub.com

E-mail: info@bookleafpub.com

ISBN: 9789358319033

First edition 2023

for everyone who got me here.

PREFACE

I'd like to think I sacrificed a lot for this book. Not because I want to have given up the time I could've spent writing English essays, or all the italics I used in my original document (the online form seems to not like formatting), but because concepts like sacrifice and devoting yourself to a challenge you know you might not be able to complete makes everything feel more profound.
I am always looking for things to be profound. Through run-on sentences and titles of poems, I constantly find myself looking for meaning in whatever world we live in. And I do not claim to know anything about the human condition. I am eighteen years old and I am an amateur everything and all I want to do here is write out some of the words that intertwine themselves with whatever I've got rattling inside my bones. I admit I did not look up how to write a preface (or what exactly a preface even is) before writing this. I seem to find myself in that position quite a bit — barreling into something without reading the instructions. But how, even, does one instruct poetry? How do you even begin to tell someone what to do with the voices

in their head, the thoughts strung together on garlands, the only constant among the chaos? That is a rhetorical question for me as well—I do not know its answer.

Whoever you are, whatever role you have in this book and its journey: I seek to do nothing to your mind. I cannot hope for influence in the eyes of a stranger, and I'm afraid to build myself up to the point where I ever could hope like that. I just want to tell you some sort of story about some sort of person who got it in their head that they could do this. I think it's more up to you than me to decide if my mad little mind actually got there.

This is a short book, something small, something trembling and scared, but it's got a part of me embedded deep inside, peeking through the pages. I think it wants some company.

conscious

i can't manage to get the words out of my mind
but i can't put them together either.
i'm scrambling to reach deadlines
but my eyes won't dry
and my compromise is
sitting at the edge of the water trying to feel
human.
i have some grandiose idea for how this is all
going to go
but the truth is i am just a lonely child with too
many tears.
i do not know where i'm going
i'm trying to live in the moment but it's going
too fast
(the truth is i'm sprinting until things slow
down)
(the truth is i'm spinning until i drown)
i am not gone yet.
i want to turn this world into something better
(do you see the grandiose now)
i want to change everything i find
and i don't know if that's the grass not being
green enough
or if it truly is a result of this world being so
hateful

so broken
so strongly delved into everything that hollows
us until we're shattered little shells
is that what i am?
i know this is stream of consciousness i know
this is just an unsteady route through my mind
i am too selfaware and i'm still just a kid with
nothing going for me
so forgive me if these words do not make sense.

this is how i write poetry

i am sitting in a car alone with a plush lavender
hoodie slung over my shoulders
and my neck is craned just enough to make me
worried for my spine
and it's cold and my shoes aren't on right and it
is 7:14 in the morning
and this is how i write poetry.
unremarkable. grasping gasping for mundanity
because
everything changes
i can just about see the dawn over the waves
(ferryboat) but it sparks
nothing
in me
it is nice on my eyes and it stops in the sockets
it does not reach whatever part of me makes
these words (brain/soul/otherwise)
oh these words. oh how they have changed me.
oh how small i would be without them.
i would not be here if i hadn't started all this
writing.
i haven't been writing lately
and whenever this happens i get scared that the
poetry is done with me

i know i know it's stupid it's a little silly i know
things don't work like that.
i just relocated myself. i say this as an apology
to the moment that i have left interrupted
and waiting for the end of these lines—
i do not expect to tie up all my loose ends. i have
left myself scattered across state lines
—and something about that is so sad (but it
sounds so nice)—
i have left myself scattered across state lines and
i shed fragments everywhere i go
fragments of my heart of my soul and i think it's
so funny so something that
in poetry i believe in souls.
i am a skeptic when i try and something else
when i don't
but i have never walked around believing that
there is some essence in us
that outlives our weakest breaths. and i want to
give everyone who hasn't met me
a precautionary note
that i am not what i make myself out to be. i
stumble over sentences and i am barely sane
at best
and sometimes the world falls apart in my mind
and my thrashing lungs feel the backlash
sometimes
i just want the world to stop.
and that is when i write poetry.

when i'm either choking on whatever's supposed
to heal me or i'm
holding tight the words that got me through hell
or i'm just
sitting at a table alone with my thin black hoodie
zipped up to my throat
and it's so damn cold out that i'm worried for
my extremities
and it's dark and my shoes are coming off and it
is 7:05 in the evening
and this
is how i write
poetry.

externalworldskepticism

for reality to exist we must be part of it
elaborate: for anything to be functional as part of
our existence
we must be aware of its existence otherwise
we have no reality
elaborate: if you see me
and then you close your eyes
and then you open them again
i am still there. or i am there again.
you have no way to tell between reality
crumbling and collapsing in a millisecond
versus
everything unchanged.
you do not know
where the world goes when you blink you do not
know if we are all figments of your imagination
(you've got a whole universe flitting through
your axons)
for reality to exist
you've got to define reality in the first place
but senses are perspective and perception is
subjective
and you never really know what's going on
outside that skull of yours

and maybe i'm just scared of my world not
being real
and maybe i'm just finding a home in hume's
philosophies because
it makes more sense than all of us being
individuals
i don't know what i'm grasping at.
i don't know what i'm trying to say here i just
know that my mind might be
the end the beginning the only definition of
reality
but how could i come up with these words these
ideas these colors these concepts
how could i create something so grand as what i
look at here and now:
all the realities we've got here looking in our
eyes
all the things that didn't last and all the things
that haven't stayed
how could i make this up? how could i create
this
mayhem this mockery of our planet this
everything i think too much
i think too much
but i don't think it's enough to fill this space.

oil and water

because i don't believe in god i have too many
questions and not enough answers
and i think
i know
that even if i did believe in something someone
up there
i might not have the most accurate outlook and i
don't want to be rude i'm just saying
we can't all be right
can we?
and because i don't think destiny is real i just
might suffer the brunt of karma
or maybe it slides by because oil and water don't
exist in each other's worlds
and i think we've all got pocket universes where
our own truth is
and i wonder what mine looks like.
i don't want to paint a picture of hypotheticals
because i was never really good with either
but i do wonder what it would look like to step
into my brain
as someone who's never been there before.
this poem is the low rumble of a machine in the
distance.

it's background noise to fill up time and maybe
it bothers you
but most of the time you're just oblivious to its
function
(if it has one)
and because i have commitment issues i can
never stick to one belief
i used to go to church when i was young just
because i wanted to
and maybe it was an extension of needing
community i don't know
maybe i just wanted to try it out
and then for a while i was an orthodox atheist
because
it didn't make sense for us to all be marionettes
like who has that many hands?
now i guess i'm just agnostic but labels aren't
my thing anymore i think
there are experiences that really do transcend
simplicity
life is so strange and i think we know so little
about everything
that we could perfectly well be living under the
gaze of some cosmic entity
or in a computer program coded on the
imaginary plane
i said i don't believe in god and i don't
i'm more one for evolution because it makes
sense to me

but i'm trying to retrain myself to not point and
laugh
at the people who find sense somewhere else.
look if you're not hurting anyone any more than
you have to if you want to coexist with pain
then i don't really have a problem with your
cosmological difference in music taste.

confidants

you tell me how you think i'm confident.
and i am honored that you believe that.
i was never very good at façades so i'm really
happy i can now display myself to be
anyone/everyone i'm not.
i am not confident. i am a bottle of fading luck
and i am fully aware of that.
you tell me how you think i got this and i am
proud of myself for convincing you so harshly
that i am not dependent on everything that
makes the world go round/backwards/sideways
upside down.
to sound a little more academic. if you will.
(tryhard)
i am filled with disbelief at the mere suggestion
that i have anything going for me. because
i do not.
i do not.
i do not have anything in terms of 1. confidence
2. competence 3. comfort i am uncomfortable in
my own skin and here we are again. with the
scars and the freckles and the dirt under my
fingernails and the buzzing brainwave that i take
up too much space.
maybe that's what the confidence (projected) is.

maybe it's just me trying to fill as much space
with my ego as i do with my body.
but thoughts don't follow conservation of mass
my brain can be as big as i want it to
and i can think as hard as loud as much as i want
yet—poetry is an extension of my brain. poetry
is where my thoughts go
when they're feeling romantic and lonely and
charming
seeking out some lover. anyone. from the
realizations and hypotheses in these pixels
to the broken hearts of anyone who looks at
them the right way.
we are all subjective. we are all holding worlds
in our souls.
you cannot call me confident just because i
sweep my insecurity under the rug.
i imagine my pain as the sun. it brings its own
opposite on by pure illusion.
you cannot say that night is the absence of day.
nothing is ever dark. day will live on
and the sun will always come back. always rise.
always hurt you if you try to confront it.
(remember i said it was just like my pain)
you tell me how you think i'm eloquent. how a
what a way with words i have.
you might not be listening to the times i speak.
i am no performer. i am no paragon of steadiness
or cohesivity. i am someone who

stumbles/mumbles/stutters/mutters oh i like that
quadratic so much.
this is why i type. this is why i turn a blank page
into lovely little beauties
that make you think i'm the same as them.
but i am not. i am not good at talking and i am
not good at smiling and i am not good at
existing in a diminished chord.
the only thing i'm good at is writing.
writing and writing and
writing well enough to convince you i'm
someone worth reading.

paper in hands

i long to be held.
i long to be cradled in some hopeful soul's
hands,
wonderent fingers seeking home in the pages.
i long for these words to be found.
desperation, you say.
trying, is my protest.
i am not the sort who writes my own story. i am
the sort who lets the world write it for me.
and i don't mean fate i do not believe in destiny i
do not believe in the unchanged—
or the unchangeable.
i believe in the art of collecting fragments of
souls
and putting them together
and filling in the gaps with words
kintsugi, you call it.
poetry, i refute.
i long to walk into the bookstore on some foggy
autumn day
and see myself on the shelves i forever pluck
paperbacks from.
and see my words.
vanity, you accuse.
i don't fight back on that one.

3040 miles

i kick my feet like a child when you say you'll
always love me
i've never gotten this love before. i'm aching to
write something more profound
than this
but philosophy doesn't make me smile like you
do. usually.
i have never liked the human body. i have never
looked at it and felt anything
but awe at all the little intricacies woven
together.
i am not attracted to the world the way every
poet seems to be.
i do not want to be with you the way everyone
wants to be with everyone else.
and i know you know that.
and i know you know that
you have clouded those facts a little bit
blurred your fair share of lines
you are special.
and i love how you think i am too
because i never thought i was and i could say
that a thousand times and still
not communicate how absently i looked at
myself.

i once used the word abhor and i didn't like it
because it didn't feel like enough
why am i crying right now? why are my hands
shaking?
probably because everything made me feel like
that back then.
tearstained shivering empty cold
but this is not about me. for once.
this is about how my shirt smells like you and
i'm drowning in it
this is about how you are still three thousand
miles away from me
this is about how i miss you
and i cannot communicate in that simple
statement how much you mean to me
you mean so much to me. you are so much to
me.
you negate the hatred i've harbored for myself
for absolute years
and you are something more than what i was
looking for all that time.
you are something more than what i wanted.
what i thought i needed you are what you have
always been:
someone who found her way between my
stumbles and caught me every time i fell
someone who redefined me someone who
understood me understands me

and we know you weren't alone in all that but
damn if you didn't save me too.

memory journal

i had a journal once.
you know, the kind
you buy from the book section in target and you
have to fill in the prompts?
5 year memory journal! watch your growth! fill
in every day for five goddamn years!
who can do that shit i swear
but i had a good thing going
until
1. i lost it
2. my world fell apart (i think)
(i mean it's happened so many times that i don't
know what the standard is anymore)
3. i didn't go looking for it after my vision
stopped spinning and everything
righted itself
to be clear: i don't write in it anymore. i don't
really know where it is and i think it'd be a
waste
of time to look back on all the bad days
(when they're already nesting in my head)
i think it's a good reflection of
something
some metaphor is aching for life right now and
(i've never had that feeling) i can't find it.

yes. i have grown.
i have taken steps i have changed i have looked
back and sat down and sobbed i am human
what do you expect i mean really
another point to make:
i have written so much about who i used to be
i have said those godforsaken pronouns so much
and the funny part is they don't hurt me
i mean it makes sense like why would someone
else's words get under my skin? i say that
and i realize what i'm implying (sticks and
stones) and i very nearly
laugh
at all this because besides why am i writing a
poem about something that
doesn't affect me anymore?
(yet—doesn't it?)
goddamnit why do i have to find paragraphs in
phrases
why do i have to turn sentences into speeches
honestly why am i doing this at all?

i had a journal once.
and i thought i would have the most normal five
years i thought i'd be fine at the end of it
(as if that ever risked a chance)
and
look at me now.

look at all of this anger. all of this fear. all of the
words cradled in my cupped palms.
look at me now.
look at my anger. look at my fear. look at all of
the words stuck beneath my bitten fingernails.
do you really think i could fit this all in a book?

patchwork/carrion

i think
i must have once
said that old saying about sticks and bones and
words
words can never hurt me
is that a fact then
or am i just really really trying to make it one
words are my armor (even if i forget what the
fight is)
i wear crushed-up-flower-bud
sunset-warm-color war-paint
i stumble over my unrhyming battle cry
not because i think too fast
just because my words want to be free so bad
and the dovetails cluttering my throat
break into disjointed song all by themselves
that was too poetic for this moment
it is 11:41 at night and i'm overheating under my
blanket and my phone screen is
that much too bright
and the door's wide open and it smells like gull
shit and seaweed
but it's close enough to safe in here.
i wrote a lie
in a poem

not that long ago
and i wouldn't say 'haunt' is the way to go about
this but it's doing something to my brain
circling like i'm patchwork carrion
but i said
for some reason
claimed that my poems are not kind.
yet they are. they are kinder than the rest of me.
they are the fragile gentle truths and half-truths
that escape through my fingers
my fingers: because my mouth does little better
than mangle even the prettiest words
(especially the prettiest words)
i hate my voice.
i hate the way i talk.
and how it's too fast and sometimes not even i
can keep up with myself
so i screech to a halt and tumble over myself
until i forget the shame ever left me.
and do you get what i mean when i say my
poems are kind?
it's not because i walk away from the truth it's
not because i sugarcoat it
(per se)
it's just because i find a new way to look at
things
through the petals of a rose
through the silver of a cloud

through the lens of a smile i don't mean that i
am unkind in real life
(i'd have to be able to talk to reach that level)
all i mean is that i am sometimes the words
come out
through my fingers or my teeth or maybe if i
know you well enough—my eyes
and i am lonelier than i let on and i am more
aware of everything than i should be
and the lies fall right out along with the secrets.
i am kind. i am kinder than i think i understand
even on my best days.
but my poems are better than that. i think.
i hope.

if only

my world is: watching gesticulation from the
backseat with my headphones on
& i am the fly on the wall.
wondering how anyone makes any sense of this
while i'm not even a part of it in the first place.
i have always set myself apart. if only to avoid
what they will always do to me (leave)
—but maybe just because i don't want to get
involved.
i don't want to make friends anymore. i'm good
with where i am & i'm scared
if i give my trust to anyone more then i'll shatter
into little pieces
& get mopped up by the people with the robotic
smiles & the barely words.
do not walk past me. if only because i've heard
those steps too many times.
muffled by mottled brown carpeting. do not
leave. if only because i ask.
i think someone got a few letters wrong when
they programmed me.
i think someone thought i'd get my shit together
at some point
& endearing as that thought is
i have not.

i see myself in the words caught in my throat i
see myself in the clouds covering the sun
poignant for a moment but makes a pretty
desolate lifetime
& we are all fighting to get through this. & i do
not underestimate myself.
if only because there's no more rock bottoms to
reach.

reflection of a former self

what a strange thing it is that i want to write a
poem
about a poem that i wrote.
sometimes i write so hard that a realization falls
out of my fingers
you'd think i'd have carpal tunnel by now
what power it is to write a line and return to it
over and over. again.
do you think that's why she hurt so much?
because no one wanted her to stay forever?
it hurts me too
i've written to her so many times
but that maybetruth is unavoidable now.
it truly is something to think about. it is.
do you think (you, who never met her) she really
did know?
do you think (you, who never saw her cry) (you
might be the only one) she was so
trapped in the present
that she saw the future instead?
do you think do you think do you think i am still
her?
i don't know who else i would be.
but whatever happened
no matter what happened

she did change. she did move on from herself.
and i think she might've realized how broken
she was.
i think
i think
it might've been more obvious than i'm
suggesting
more clear to tearwashed eyes than these words
imply.
the truth is this—
she was in so much pain\
no one. no one wanted that person to be who she
was forever.
(wish come true)
and now. as i type in her bed in her room in her
house. (nothing changed) (everything did)
i realize for the thousandth time since writing
that line
that we talk about her. we talk about how it's so
good it's such a relief that
she is gone.
but imagine that being your future.
imagine living through so much. too much for
your heart to handle
and here's my mind again undermining that
trauma
imagine breaking. imagine breaking and imagine
your future being
healing &

loving &
smiling &
making jokes about who you used to be.
i cannot enunciate enough what pain that brings
me i cannot divide between relief and malicion
i cannot tell her i still love her.

broken words/better days

you look at me
and i don't actually know what you see i don't
want to put words in your mouth
and hell,
i don't actually know if you even see me at all
but if you do
look through all the people whose stories we'll
never know
and fix your eyes on mine
i will tell you my story.
i will tell you about my fragile little self
and how i'm too scared and too stuck in the past
(and the future)
and how i think i'm an absolutely horrible poet
but i do think i'm very unique.
which is what the kids get told when everyone
wants to sugarcoat their lonely
or 'gifted' when your parents don't know how to
tell you that you're smart in the wrong way
and i know i am young. i am eighteen going on
postmortem and maybe you don't think
that i can be a poet right now. and maybe you
read these words and you don't think
that i can be a poet ever.

but i don't write these words to appease you. (i
hope)
i am not writing this to sound middle aged with
a college degree
shit, don't you think i'd add capitals for that?
no.
i know exactly how unprofessional i am. i know
exactly how scared i am that
no one will ever find me and my words and all
the aspirations i'm dying to have
(i live to live but i never actually get there)
i am writing in my room listening to some song
that can't save me anymore—but how it did.
and i am feigning composure to the
shadows—but i promise i took my meds today.
and at some point tonight she'll call me—but for
right now the poems have my love.

not falling together
(etymology)

we are as an asymptote does
(and isn't that such a pretty word?)
we are split/severed/separate
over graph lines
over miles and miles and
over three thousand miles—in fact.
and i will be brutal here.
and i will be honest here.
it fucking hurts i swear there are times when i
don't know what to
do with myself is it the overreacting that
everyone tells me i do
or is this what you get when you fall in love so
frequent so fast so helplessly far
i am drop dead disembodied with my ringer on
and my brain melting through my tear ducts
and i am screamsobbing to the bathroom tiles
"how the fuck do i do this"
as if i didn't get into this knowing just how
much you mean to me
and just how hardly i will attach myself to
someone who lives in an other time zone
what am i looking for? what am i looking at?

tearstricken face in the bathroom mirror and i
just want to be in your arms.

we are as an asymptote does. in all truth i forgot
the theme i was going for here
until i read the first line and i have been wanting
to write a poem about those little
lines for months now i should do this concept
some justice and i am
scared. i am scared that concept is all you will
ever be
rephrase you are real you are so so real i know
that
but you have become a screen and i'm not trying
to strain my eyes with your existence
—my heart's already strained enough

since numbers are the concreteness that keeps
me alive when my emotions are all tied up in
slipperyslopeslipknots
since atoms never really touch each other
since i am forever reaching out for our school
breaks to coincide
since i am maybe asking for things you are just
not able to give me
since i am here and you are there
then/thus/therefore
we are as an asymptote does.

found poetry: 1923
newspapers

there was a light breeze.
nothing to gouge the flesh—but by all means
make a move.
optimism prevails,
its wings giving away in the face of a stiff wind.

search was abandoned today.
the delusion of both sides was short lived
as each night for months proceeding
every hungry mouth and heart
lowered his gaze from the heavens.

a house built of separate blocks of granite.

kaleidoscopic changes.

student of the stars (face worked
spasmodically—with a look of inexpressible
scorn)
he is a sort of pale, dreaming philosopher.

there was something infinitely pathetic
in a heart which has been stilled by death.
in the mystery of a silence.

we have a way of brushing aside the grief of
others as something remote.

we are all poets.

we are all poets.
we are all children looking up at the stars
waiting for one to fall into the bowl of our
outstretched hands
so we can carry it home and show the world
what we've found.

we are all poets.
we are all children looking up at the trees
waiting for a leaf to drift into the air right beside
us
so we can claim to be the first thing it's ever
fallen on.

we are all poets.
we are all children looking up at a plane
waiting for someone to wave back
so we can say that we were noticed from miles
away.

we are all poets.
we are all ghosts looking out through the veil
waiting to know if we've been mourned or not
because we just want to be special

we are all poets we feel so hard so strong
and we don't know what to do with it
but expel it from ourselves.
we are all poets we are lost we are found we are
somewhere
in between we are something

and for the sake of whatever can we just feel
special for once?

speechless and intelligent and shaking with shame (post-howl)

i write this having read so much
let me be your darling if i cannot ask that much
of the world
of my past
of my fears
i write this with ginsberg's voice storming still
in my broken molten mind
everything stays a little past the midnight hour
everything hovers. waiting for me to transcribe
my own interpretations
as if i'm some godly prophet with nothing to
believe in and nowhere to hide
i write this having seen something i don't look at
the little uglies of our world the anger and the
shame
the skulls smashed open the hearts caved in
we are all dying and i am buzzing with potential
energy
(does it mean something that i first wrote that as
poet)
i read it again. but this time i'm aching to write
more of my own creation

to chase the words down and corner them until
they let me and my impulsive destructive anger
turn them into museum pieces
(the museum being a backalley backroad
building full of people looking for a better
tomorrow)
i see myself in the mirror. i see you in my
thoughts. i see better tomorrows in twenties
papers
and i see beauty in the words. the words.
i go back to it. dip my quill in the ink again.
restart refresh i pick up the wrong book but let's
see
let's see what's inside
seven minutes pass.
nonsense. nonsensical and it's not quite as
profound as the first one but i feel the
run on sentences and superfluous adjectives
coming back full force
i want to have such a mind.
words are stumbling now in my mind ebbing
flowing ebbed all the way now
and i really do feel like i'm mimicking genius
with this. mimicking i will never be anyone but
a lost little soul with a broken heart and brains
don't develop fully until you're 25 anyway
that is to say i've got seven years left
9 10 11 12 1 2 3 4 5 goes the counting on my
fingers and i can't figure out why 9 isn't right

brains don't develop fully until you're 25
anyway.

rhyme scheme

i've found that i don't like rhyming poems
i mean it's a good start
when you're in elementary school
and you don't know who you are
but you do know words
and what if you arranged them this way?
just so?
but children's rhymes are clunky
and not precise
like a toddler playing with blocks
poetry is so much more than assonance and mix
and match
and i don't mean to say you can't rhyme if you
really want to
and maybe i'm just complaining because i find it
hard sometimes
to make the next word fit
but i can take this to a deeper level
(like i do everything i mean like if i have a
specialty)
and talk about rigidity and structure and how
i don't want to constrain this bit of my soul that
finds its way onto the page
and if i'm going to trap it in between words

they will not be words that are halfheartedly
pulled tight together
by a concept i've long let go of
they will be the pretty ones and the ones that
mean something on their own
they will be the strong ones.

kids of summer

we washed up on the shores of that lake
slash pond
i mean whatever they want to call it
we washed up on the shores of that lake
unknowing and unclear and unhappy
and i know i'm projecting but godforbid it was
just me
we washed up on the shores of that lake
on that day in late june
and we found each other.
the four of us
this motley crew
full of dreams not realized and sins not wreaked:
12. 13. 13. 14.
you can call age just a number but we were kids
then
oh we were.
we were children and i think we were all a little
broken even then
but maybe the ruptures lend themselves better to
healing
and you could've told me we would stay like
that forever
and i would've believed you in a heartbeat.

yet. maybe that's just my hope breaking through.
maybe that's just the absence of pain
translating to the absence of change.
maybe it is.
i could've stayed in that summer for the rest of
time. i really could have.
but time goes on and the world keeps pirouetting
around the sun like a prima
and nothing stays.
and nothing stays and nothing stays and i am
still aching for what we had back then
because we are not four people anymore.
we are three
and i still wish i had the courage to reach out and
talk to the one who unattached
and tell her she will always be a part of me
because it's true.
i digress to another truth:
there is a song that makes me cry every time i
hear it.
it is called kids of summer and i swear to
everything it breaks me.
i wonder if you remember those days with the
joy that i do. even though they were not joyful
they were strange and they were fearful and they
were lonely even in the best moments.
that is how i work i find emptiness in our
crowded world and there is a lonely beneath my
smiles.

i smile, despite that. i smile at our good old days.
i smile at how we found each other and
refused to let go.
i hope we always refuse. to stop grasping for
accompanism in this murky swamp of life.
to never ever unhold each other close because
this time we've found someone who can't leave.
who we won't allow to leave.
we're all holding each other hostage and i've
never felt more loved or lovely.

it's not that deep

i think my heart stopped.
i think it was your fault.
i have already written the best poem i could
about you
and i have already rid my mind of your face
too many times to count
but it always comes back. you always come
back. you still come back
and i don't know what to do
what do i tell her?
there is no prettiness found in the confession that
i wrote thousands of words for you
and i still think you're beautiful
and i dreamt of your eyes a few nights ago
and you will always be the fairytale i didn't get.
you were so much to me. and i cannot say
goodbye because
you didn't say it first
and i can't end anything that's not worth ending
what do i tell her?
how do i communicate to the person i would do
anything for
the person i love more than i can possibly reason
out
that there was someone who got there first?

who broke me by making my heart a little bigger
expanding stretched and taut until it ripped apart
and you will always be a part of me. that is so
so terrifying and i want you to leave.
i want you to get the love i almost gave you
from someone who will not get scared
someone who will not be the wrong one for you
while you're the right one for them
(the first right one that they have ever met)
and the worst part is i think she would
understand.
i think she would tell me she still loved me
no matter who crept into my mind sometimes.
and even if she didn't
even if these things didn't happen
she is still too good for me
and you
are still too good for me
this is simpler than i intended. these murmurs
are much more mundane
than i wanted from any poem.
i do not think you are simple. and isn't that the
least interesting part of this all?
that i think you are quite exceptional and i really
really do believe that
you deserve for the world to see you that way.
even if your world is someone else.

things no one told me

you are allowed to love the people who hurt you.
you are allowed to be weak.
you are allowed to not do your best.
you are allowed to cry in public.
you are allowed to regret your actions.
you are allowed to not regret your actions.
you are allowed to be wrong.
you are allowed to need help.
you are allowed to tell on people.
you are allowed to walk away.
you are allowed to overreact.
you are allowed to exist.

all art is quite useless
(questions)

where do you read this?
i have so many questions for you.
do you read this firsthand off my screen as i sit
behind you and devour it ruthlessly
do you hear it in the room that i hope means
something someday?
(a beginning, of sorts)
do you see it in a book
or on a website
or does someone else show it to you?

and i guess i want to know who you are.
not because i think there is anyone unworthy of
what i make
(i don't place the value here, not now)
i picture you
you nameless faceless soul
bursting with everything no one can tamp down
i picture you
at a table. with your coffee or your tea or some
other refined, intellectual beverage.
and there are papers rustling in the breeze
through the window and

you don't really know why the window's open
anyway.
it's not summer anymore. but you are covered in
ink stains because you're going too fast
and you're always in a rush but poetry makes
you calm down sometimes.
i picture you in a bookstore.
and you're trying to find a book that doesn't
have that one texture
that all poets seem to use these days
i promise you it bothers me too.
but what doesn't bother you are the words laid
out in a font that i really hope is pretty
and i guess i'm a people pleaser yeah that makes
sense.

i have so many questions.
i want to know your name. your favorite color.
i want to know what song you played on repeat
the other day.
i want to know what you think of thunderstorms
in summer and
how long you've hated that one thing about
yourself.
that you think stands out to everyone but might
just not.
i want to know what you think i'm like and i
can't wait to tell you you're wrong

because i am not ethereal. i am not eloquent. i
talk too fast and i stumble over my sentences
and i'm constantly repeating myself and i hate
getting interrupted so no,
i am not good with words. in case you were
wondering.
on the good days i'm pretty and on the bad days
i'm tired and those
are by no means mutually exclusive but i don't
know. sometimes it feel otherwise and
i don't really know why.

but i still have so many questions and none of us
have enough time
so i'll give you your peace.
someone's got to have some.

9 789358 319033